Essential

FRENCH
COOKERY

Essential
FRENCH
COOKERY

CHANCELLOR
PRESS

First published in Great Britain in 1994 by Chancellor Press
an imprint of Reed Consumer Books Limited
Michelin House, 81 Fulham Road, London SW3 6RB
and Auckland, Melbourne, Singapore and Toronto

Designed and produced by SP Creative Design
Linden House, Kings Road, Bury St Edmunds, Suffolk, England
Editor and writer: Heather Thomas
Art Director: Al Rockall
Designer: Rolando Ugolini

ISBN 1 85152 664 1

A CIP catalogue record for this book is available from the
British Library

Printed in Spain by Cayfosa, Barcelona.

Acknowledgements

Special photography: Laurie Evans
Step-by-step photography: GGS Photographics, Norwich
Food preparation: Janice Murfitt and Dawn Stock
Styling: Lesley Richardson

Notes

1. Standard spoon measurements are used in all recipes.
1 tablespoon = one 15ml spoon
1 teaspoon = one 5ml spoon

2. Both imperial and metric measurements have been
given in all recipes. Use one set of measurements
only and not a mixture of both.

3. Eggs should be size 3 unless otherwise stated.

4. Milk should be full fat unless otherwise stated.

5. Fresh herbs should be used unless otherwise stated.
If unavailable, use dried herbs as an alternative, but halve the
quantities stated.

6. Ovens should be preheated to the specified temperature.
If using a fan assisted oven, follow the manufacturer's
instructions for adjusting the time and the temperature.

CONTENTS

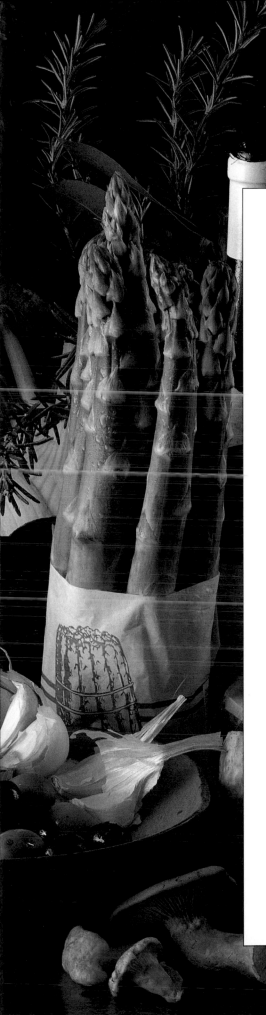

INTRODUCTION

French cookery is one of the world's great cuisines, with many classic regional dishes which have evolved over the centuries. There are two traditions running through French cooking: *la haute cuisine,* as practised by the great chefs and restaurants; and *la cuisine régionale,* which consists of the natural regional specialities utilizing the best local and seasonal ingredients.

The food of France reflects the climate and geography of the country, from the exotic and colourful dishes of sun-soaked Provence to the creamy sauces of Normandy and the Ile de France. The cooking of the north – Flanders, Artois and Picardy – is simple, hearty and wholesome; from the north-eastern region of Alsace and Lorraine come pâtés and dishes made with game, freshwater fish, bacon and cheese. Normandy and Brittany, in the north-west of France, are renowned for their fresh fish and shellfish, apples, cider, cream and dairy produce.

Further south along the fertile banks of the River Loire, lie the vineyards, orchards and cornfields of Touraine, Anjou, Orléanais and Maine. These regions are famous for their pork dishes, fruit tarts and pies. From the mountainous centre of France, Auvergne and Limousin, come rustic country dishes of root vegetables, charcuterie, mushrooms and trout, while the Rhône-Alps, Bourgogne, Lyonnais, Dauphine and Savoie provide the highly prized truffles, tender beef and delicious cheeses.

The Atlantic seaboard – Aquitaine, Bordeaux, Perigord and Gascogne – is notable for its fresh seafood, foie gras and Armagnac, one of France's finest brandies. From the warm south, stretching from Toulouse in the west through the Languedoc-Rousillon to Provence and the Côte d'Azur, come distinctive dishes of fish, meat and poultry flavoured with juicy tomatoes, peppers, aubergines, garlic, aromatic herbs and fruity olive oil.

The French love to eat, and everywhere you go in France you will find exquisite food, prepared and cooked with infinite care from only the finest and freshest ingredients. With the exception of the north, where cider and beer are sometimes served, wine is the indispensable accompaniment to every meal. The local wines and the vins ordinaire (everyday table wines) form the basis of many famous dishes, such as Coq au Vin and Boeuf à la Bourguignonne.

FRENCH INGREDIENTS

Bouquet garni

This is a small bundle of herbs, usually sprigs of fresh parsley and thyme and a bay leaf which are tied together with string or thread. It is used to flavour stocks, soups, stews and casseroles and is immersed in the cooking liquid, and removed later before serving.

Cheeses

France is justly famous for its huge array of regional and locally produced cheeses of which there are literally hundreds. Each individual cheese has its own special texture, flavour and character, which makes it unique. Cheeses are used in cooking, and the cheeseboard is an important ritual in most meals. It is served before the dessert and a wide range of cheeses are offered. Some of the best-known French cheeses are as follows:

Brie: this is a creamy soft cheese from the Ile de France, which is best eaten when really ripe and runny.

Camembert: this soft cheese hails from Normandy and has a stronger flavour and aroma than Brie. It should also be served when it is ripe and is best consumed at room temperature, never straight out of the refrigerator.

Chèvre: most regions have their own local goat's milk cheeses, which are usually soft in texture with a strong distinctive flavour.

Gruyère: widely used in cooking, this cheese has a firm texture and a nutty, slightly salty flavour. It is made in the mountainous region of Savoie and is excellent for grating.

Roquefort: this is regarded by cheese afficionados as the king of cheeses. Blue-veined, semi-hard, with a creamy, crumbly texture, Roquefort is made from ewe's milk and is aged in the underground caves of the Saint-Affrique district in central France.

Confit d'oie

Traditionally used in cassoulet, this speciality of preserved goose, which has been cooked in goose fat, comes from south-western France. It can be purchased at most good delicatessens and specialist food stores.

Foie gras

This is held in high esteem by the French who regard it as the greatest of all culinary delicacies. Foie gras is the liver of specially fattened geese, and the finest ones come from Alsace and south-western France. The geese are fattened up in such a way that their livers grow to a considerable size. Foie gras is traditionally used in making pâté but it is also sometimes baked in brioche dough or used as a filling for crêpes and croquettes, or sliced and sautéed in butter.

Garlic

This is an essential ingredient in many French dishes, especially those of Provence and the south of the country. It is used as a flavouring in many soups, stews and casseroles, and is the essential ingredient in the great Provençal pistou sauce, which is stirred into a soup of beans and vegetables just before serving. Cut cloves of garlic are often rubbed around the inside of a salad bowl before adding the salad leaves to impart a subtle flavour and aroma to the salad. Likewise, they can be rubbed around an earthenware gratin dish before making a gratin of potatoes or other vegetables.

Herbs

Most savoury dishes are flavoured and scented with the aromatic leaves of at least one herb. Chervil, tarragon, parsley and chives are the most frequently used ones, but rosemary, basil and fennel are popular and, indeed, essential in many southern dishes. They may be tied together in a small bundle (bouquet garni) or chopped. They are added to omelettes, sauces, soups, stews, casseroles, grilled meat, poultry and fish. Fresh herbs are preferable to dried ones. You can buy them in most supermarkets or grow them yourself in the garden or in pots on your kitchen windowsill.

Chives: the long onion-flavoured leaves of chives are snipped with scissors and added to salads, omelettes, soups and sauces.

Parsley: sprigs may be used in a bouquet garni, or they can be chopped and used as a flavouring or as a garnish before serving.

Tarragon: this typically French herb is used to flavour many classic sauces, especially bearnaise sauce, omelettes and green salads. It can be steeped in wine vinegar to make vinaigre à l'estragon, which is used in sauces and salad dressings.

Thyme: the small leaves of this pungent herb are used for flavouring many soups, stews and casseroles.

Mushrooms

In France, many varieties of mushrooms are used in cooking – not just the small button cultivated ones. Wild mushrooms are highly prized, especially cèpes, chanterelles and morilles (morels). They are used in a wide range of dishes, and may be cooked in cream with herbs, or added to salads and sauces, or used as a filling for vol-au-vent cases and crêpes, or simply grilled or cooked au gratin.

Mustard

The most famous and widely used mustard is moutarde de Dijon, which is flavoured with white wine and tarragon.

However, the mustards of Bordeaux and Meaux are also popular. Mustard is used as a flavouring in many sauces, and is mixed with olive oil and vinegar in salad dressings. All French mustards are sold ready mixed in bottles as a paste, not in powdered form

Olive oil

This is made by pressing ripe olives and is essential for making authentic vinaigrette salad dressings, mayonnaise, aioli and rouille. Olive oil is an essential ingredient in many dishes from Provence, unlike the cookery of the north where butter is widely used instead. The finest and purest oil is extracted cold from the best ripe olives and is green and fruity. However, it is expensive and you can buy cheaper alternatives, although they will not have the same flavour and aroma

Olives

These are characteristic of southern French cookery, and are used in many ways: as a garnish, in stuffings and sauces, and most notably in tapenade and daubes, the distinctive stews of Provence.

Onions

These deserve a special mention because they are used so extensively in French cookery: in sauces, tarts, casseroles, stews and classic dishes like soupe à l'oignon and pissaladière. A variety of onions are used from the tiny pickling onions and shallots to large mild onions, red skinned ones and the tender shoots of spring onions.

Snails

Known in France as escargots, snails can be cooked fresh in wine or stock with various herbs, shallots and vegetables for flavouring, but they are usually

purchased canned or frozen and are packed into shells with garlic or herb butter before heating and serving as an hors d'œuvre.

Wine

Wine is the natural partner of good food, and many of the world's finest wines come from France. It is an essential ingredient in many French regional dishes, but you need not use really expensive wine for cooking. A bottle of inexpensive vin ordinaire is usually suitable although some leftover good wine will elevate many dishes into new realms par excellence!

Equipment and utensils

There are a few basic items that are very useful when cooking French food. These include the following:

Bain-marie: this is a large shallow pan in which saucepans, bowls or dishes can be placed in a bath of water. The water should come halfway up the sides of the pan or dish. It is ideal for making sauces and egg custards and prevents them curdling.

Casserole: this may be earthenware (for using in the oven) or cast iron (for cooking on top of the stove). It is ideal for making stews and daubes. A flameproof casserole is excellent for frying vegetables and meat on top of the stove before adding the cooking liquid and placing in the oven for long, slow cooking.

Omelette pan: a small pan with sloping sides for making crêpes and omelettes. It may be made of copper, cast iron, steel or aluminium.

Soufflé dish: this high-sided fluted dish is usually made of white porcelain and can be used for making hot or cold soufflés.

ESCARGOTS A L'ALSACIENNE

Snails Alsace-style

1 Remove the snails from the can. Heat 25g/1oz of the butter in a frying pan and quickly fry the snails. Add the white wine and cook over high heat for 2-3 minutes until it evaporates. Add the stock and boil for 2 minutes. Leave to cool and then remove the snails, and discard the stock.

2 Cream the remaining butter in a small bowl. Mix in the garlic, chopped parsley and shallot, and the hazelnuts. Season with salt and freshly ground black pepper.

PREPARATION: 20 MINUTES
COOKING: 10 MINUTES
SERVES: 6

3 Carefully put a little of the garlic and herb flavoured butter into each snail shell. Then put a snail inside each shell and cover with a little more of the garlic butter.

36 canned snails and 36 shells
150g/5oz butter
3 tablespoons dry white wine
125ml/4 fl oz chicken stock
4 garlic cloves, crushed
50g/2oz chopped parsley
50g/2oz finely chopped shallot
50g/2oz hazelnuts, crushed
salt and freshly ground black pepper

4 Arrange all the filled snail shells on special snail dishes or in an ovenproof dish, and bake in a preheated oven at 200°C/400°F/Gas Mark 6 for 10 minutes. Serve immediately.

10

PISSALADIERE

Provençal onion and anchovy tart

1 Make the dough: dissolve the yeast in the water and set aside. Sift the flour and salt into a large mixing bowl, rub in the butter and make a well in the centre. Mix in the eggs and yeast liquid, drawing in the flour from the sides of the bowl to make a soft dough.

2 Turn out onto a lightly floured surface and knead well until the dough is smooth and elastic. Form into a ball, cover with a damp cloth and leave to rise in a warm place for about 30-45 minutes, until doubled in bulk. Meanwhile, heat 4 tablespoons of the oil and cook the onions very gently for about 30 minutes until soft and golden, stirring occasionally.

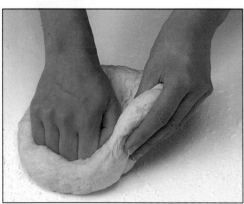

PREPARATION: 1³/₄ HOURS
COOKING: 30 MINUTES
SERVES: 6-8

3 Knock down the risen dough and knead again for a few minutes. Roll out to a circle to fit an oiled 25cm/10 inch round ovenproof plate, baking pan or mould and use to line the base. Spread the onions over the top.

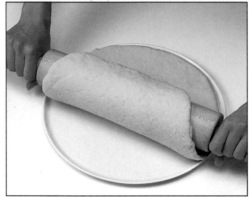

6 tablespoons olive oil
1kg/2lb onions, thinly sliced
12 canned anchovies, drained
50g/2oz black olives, halved and stoned
freshly ground black pepper
For the dough:
25g/1oz fresh yeast
4 tablespoons lukewarm water
375g/12oz plain flour
pinch of salt
50g/2oz butter, diced
2 eggs, beaten

4 Make a lattice pattern with the anchovies over the onions and decorate with the olives. Sprinkle with pepper and the remaining oil. Leave to rise in a warm place for 15 minutes. Bake in a preheated oven at 230°C/450°F/Gas Mark 8 for 30 minutes.

PATE DE CAMPAGNE

French country pâté

1 Melt the butter in a frying pan and sauté the onions and garlic gently for a few minutes until tender and golden. Transfer to a large bowl. Add the liver to the pan and fry until lightly browned. Remove and mince or chop.

2 Chop 200g/7oz of the streaky bacon and add to the bowl with the liver, pork, parsley, sage, mace, nutmeg, salt, pepper, egg whites and brandy. Mix well together until thoroughly combined.

50g/2oz butter, plus extra for greasing
2 onions, finely chopped
4 garlic cloves, crushed
500g/1lb pig's liver, diced
275g/9oz streaky bacon rashers, rind removed
500g/1lb lean pork, minced or chopped
2 tablespoons chopped fresh parsley
1/2 teaspoon dried sage
1/4 teaspoon ground mace
1/4 teaspoon ground nutmeg
salt and freshly ground black pepper
2 egg whites
2 tablespoons brandy
2 bay leaves

4 Leave the pâté to cool for 30 minutes, then cover with a piece of greaseproof paper or foil and weight lightly. Leave until completely cold and set. If wished, replace the bay leaves with fresh ones. Cover and refrigerate for about 36 hours. Serve sliced with toast or crusty bread.

3 Line a lightly greased 500g/1lb terrine or loaf tin with the remaining bacon rashers so that they hang over the sides. Fill with the pâté mixture and fold the bacon over the top. Put the 2 bay leaves on top and place in a roasting pan of hot water. Cook in a preheated oven at 190°C/375°F/Gas Mark 5 for 1½ hours, or until the juices run clear and the pâté has shrunk slightly from the sides of the tin.

PREPARATION: 30 MINUTES
COOKING: 1½ HOURS
SERVES: 8

FLAMICHE AUX POIREAUX

Leek pie

1 Make the pâte brisée: sift the flour and salt into a large mixing bowl. Cut the butter into small dice and rub into the flour until the mixture resembles breadcrumbs. Stir in the egg yolk and sufficient iced water to bind the ingredients together.

2 Knead lightly on a floured surface until smooth and elastic. Cover and leave in a cool place to rest for 1 hour. Roll out two-thirds of the pastry on a floured surface and use to line a buttered 23cm/9 inch flan ring placed on a greased baking sheet.

PREPARATION: 50 MINUTES +
RESTING TIME
COOKING: 35-40 MINUTES
SERVES: 6

3 Melt the butter in a heavy pan and cook the leeks very gently until soft and melting; this takes about 30 minutes. Stir occasionally. Add the nutmeg and seasoning and leave to cool. Whisk together the egg yolks and cream and stir into the cooled leeks.

4 Pour the leek filling into the pastry shell. Roll out the remaining pastry to make a lid. Moisten the edges and cover the flan. Pinch the edges together to seal, and crimp with a fork. Decorate with leaves made from the pastry trimmings. Beat the egg yolk and water together and brush over the pastry. Bake in a preheated oven at 200°C/400°F/Gas Mark 6 for 35-40 minutes.

50g/2oz butter
1kg/2lb leeks, thinly sliced
pinch of ground nutmeg
salt and pepper
3 egg yolks
125ml/4 fl oz double cream
For the pâte brisée:
375g/12oz plain flour
pinch of salt
175g/6oz butter
1 egg yolk
4-6 tablespoons iced water
For the glaze:
1 egg yolk
1 tablespoon water

CROQUETTES DE CAMEMBERT

Camembert fritters

1 Remove the rind from the Camembert cheese. Mash the cheese with a fork in a small bowl and beat well until it is really smooth.

2 Make a roux: melt the butter in a saucepan and stir in the flour. Cook for 1–2 minutes without browning and then stir in the milk and brandy or Calvados, beating vigorously to make a smooth, thick sauce. Season with pepper and cool. Mix in the Camembert to make a firm croquette mixture.

3 Take small amounts of the cheese mixture and roll between floured hands to make cork-shaped croquettes. Beat the egg with 2 tablespoons of cold water and use to coat the croquettes.

4 Roll the croquettes at once in a mixture of flour and breadcrumbs and then deep-fry them quickly in hot oil until golden brown. Drain on absorbent kitchen paper and serve garnished with sprigs of parsley.

PREPARATION: 12–15 MINUTES
COOKING: 15–20 MINUTES
SERVES: 4

Ingredients
1 Camembert cheese, just ripe
15g/$\frac{1}{2}$ oz butter
25g/1oz flour
5 tablespoons warm milk
1 tablespoon brandy or Calvados
$\frac{1}{4}$ teaspoon freshly ground white pepper
1 egg
1 tablespoon flour and 3 tablespoons dry breadcrumbs for coating
oil for frying
For the garnish:
sprigs of parsley

SOUPE A L'OIGNON

French onion soup

1 Melt the butter in a large saucepan and add the onions and sugar. Lower the heat to a bare simmer and cook the onions very slowly for 20-30 minutes until they are soft and a really deep golden brown. Stir occasionally and take care that they cook to a good colour without burning.

50g/2oz butter
750g/1½ lb onions, thinly sliced
2 teaspoons sugar
2 teaspoons plain flour
1 litre/1¾ pints beef stock
salt and freshly ground black pepper
½ French bread stick, sliced
50g/2oz grated Gruyère cheese

2 Stir the flour into the onion mixture and cook over a very low heat for about 5 minutes, stirring well to prevent it burning or sticking to the bottom of the pan.

4 Meanwhile, toast the slices of French bread lightly on both sides. Sprinkle with the grated Gruyère cheese. Pour the soup into a hot tureen. Place a piece of toast in each serving bowl and ladle the hot soup over the top.

3 Add the beef stock and the salt and freshly ground black pepper. Turn up the heat and bring to the boil, stirring. Reduce the heat and simmer for 15-20 minutes. Taste the soup and add more salt and freshly ground black pepper if necessary.

PREPARATION: 15 MINUTES
COOKING: 1 HOUR
SERVES: 4-5

POTAGE SAINT-GERMAIN

Split pea soup

1 Place the split peas in a sieve or a colander and rinse them thoroughly under running cold water. Soak them in cold water overnight, then rinse and drain.

2 Fry the strips of pork in the butter in a large heavy saucepan. Cook over brisk heat for 5 minutes, stirring frequently. Add the carrot and onion and fry for a further 2 minutes, stirring constantly. Add the water and split peas and bring to the boil. Tie the bay leaves and celery together and lower into the pan with the garlic. Season and simmer very gently for 2 hours.

PREPARATION: 10-15 MINUTES +
SOAKING OVERNIGHT
COOKING: 2¼ HOURS
SERVES: 6

3 Discard the bay leaves and garlic. Purée the soup in a food processor or blender until it is thick and smooth – you will have to do this in batches. Return the puréed soup to the saucepan.

500g/1lb dried yellow split peas
125g/4oz boneless salt pork, cut in strips
25g/1oz butter
1 carrot, diced
1 onion, chopped
2 litres/3½ pints water
2 bay leaves
1 celery stick
1 garlic clove, peeled and bruised
salt and freshly ground black pepper
125ml/4 fl oz double cream
To garnish:
bread croûtons

4 Stir in the cream and cook very gently over low heat for a few minutes to heat through. Stir constantly and take care that the soup does not boil. Taste and adjust the seasoning if necessary. Pour into a warm tureen or individual bowls and serve garnished with croûtons.

SOUPE AU PISTOU

Vegetable soup with basil sauce

1 Put the beans in a large bowl and cover with cold water. Leave overnight or for at least 5 hours to soak. Drain the beans and transfer to a saucepan. Cover with fresh water and bring to the boil. Skim off any scum on the surface and boil for 10 minutes. Reduce the heat and simmer for 1 hour, or until tender. Drain and set aside.

2 Prepare all the vegetables: dice the carrots, leeks and celery. Skin and chop the tomatoes roughly. Peel and dice the potatoes. Top and tail the beans and cut them into 1cm/1/2 inch lengths. Trim and dice the courgettes.

3 Heat the olive oil in a large saucepan and add the carrots, leeks, celery and tomatoes. Cook gently for 2 minutes, and then add the water. Bring to the boil, then reduce the heat immediately and simmer for 15 minutes. Add the potatoes, beans, courgettes and vermicelli. Simmer for 15–20 minutes, until the pasta and all the vegetables are tender. Season with salt and pepper.

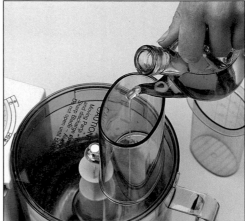

250g/8oz dried haricot beans
250g/8oz carrots
2 leeks
2 sticks celery
375g/12oz tomatoes
250g/8oz potatoes
250g/8oz thin French beans
375g/12oz courgettes
2 tablespoons olive oil
1.2 litres/2 pints water
50g/2oz vermicelli
salt and freshly ground black pepper

For the pistou:

3-4 garlic cloves, peeled
pinch of salt
20 large basil leaves
125g/4oz grated Parmesan cheese
125ml/4 fl oz olive oil

4 Make the pistou: pound the garlic cloves, salt and basil in a blender or food processor. Add the Parmesan and then pour in the olive oil in a thin trickle through the feed tube until you have a thick green paste. Stir into the soup just before serving, or hand the pistou separately.

PREPARATION: 1½ HOURS +
SOAKING TIME
COOKING: 35-40 MINUTES
SERVES: 6

TARTE A L'OIGNON

Onion tart

1 Heat the butter in a large frying pan. Add the bacon and onions and fry gently over low heat until soft and golden. Add the flour and cook for 1 minute. Stir in the milk and cream and cook for 5 minutes, stirring occasionally.

2 Remove the pan from the heat and add the egg yolks, salt, freshly ground black pepper and some freshly grated nutmeg. Stir well and then set aside to cool.

3 Roll out the pâte brisée(shortcrust pastry) on a lightly floured surface and use to line a buttered 25cm/10 inch loose-bottomed flan tin. Prick the base of the pastry with a fork.

50g/2oz butter
125g/4oz smoked bacon, diced
500g/1lb onions, finely sliced
25g/1oz plain flour
200ml/7 fl oz milk
6 tablespoons single cream
2 egg yolks
salt and freshly ground black pepper
grated nutmeg
250g/8oz pâte brisée (see page 110)

4 Pour the prepared onion mixture into the pastry case. Slide on to a baking tray and cook in a preheated oven at 180°C/350°F/Gas Mark 4 for 40 minutes, until set and golden. Serve hot.

PREPARATION: 30 MINUTES
COOKING: 40 MINUTES
SERVES: 6

SOUFFLE AU FROMAGE

Cheese soufflé

1 Make a white sauce: melt the butter in a saucepan and stir in the flour. Cook for 1-2 minutes over low heat and then gradually add the milk, stirring well between each addition, until the sauce is thick and smooth. Cook very gently for 15 minutes, stirring constantly with a wooden spoon. Remove from the heat and stir in the cream.

3 Whisk the egg whites in a clean bowl until they are really stiff, but not dry. Fold them gently into the cheese sauce mixture with a metal spoon using a figure of eight motion.

| 50g/2oz butter |
| 50g/2oz plain flour |
| 250ml/8 fl oz milk |
| 2 tablespoons cream |
| 4 egg yolks |
| 150g/5oz grated Gruyère cheese |
| salt and freshly ground white pepper |
| freshly grated nutmeg |
| 5 egg whites |

2 Stir the egg yolks into the sauce, a little at a time. Add the Gruyère cheese, salt, pepper and nutmeg to taste. Beat well until the cheese melts and the mixture is really smooth.

PREPARATION: 20 MINUTES
COOKING: 30 MINUTES
SERVES: 4

4 Transfer the mixture to a well-buttered 1.2 litre/2 pint soufflé dish or two 600ml/1 pint dishes. Bake in a preheated oven at 180°C/350°F/Gas Mark 4 for 15 minutes. Increase the temperature to 200°C/400°F/Gas Mark 6 and cook for a further 15 minutes until the soufflé is well-risen and golden. Serve immediately.

29

QUICHE LORRAINE

Savoury bacon flan

250g/8oz plain flour

pinch of salt

125g/4oz butter

1 egg yolk

2-3 tablespoons iced water

For the filling:

50g/2oz butter

150g/5oz smoked bacon, cut into small pieces

350ml/12 fl oz double cream

3 eggs

¼ teaspoon freshly grated nutmeg

salt and freshly ground black pepper

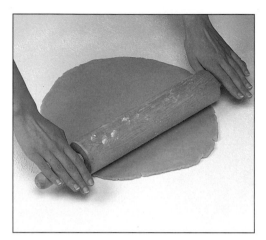

2 Roll out the pastry on a lightly floured surface and use to line a buttered 23cm/9 inch loose-bottomed flan tin. Prick the base of the flan with a fork.

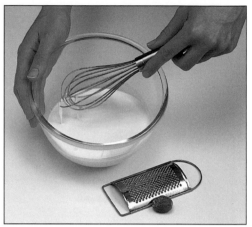

3 Melt half of the butter in a frying pan and cook the bacon pieces gently until lightly coloured. Put the cream and eggs in a bowl and whisk together. Add the grated nutmeg and seasoning.

1 Make the pastry: sift the flour and salt into a large mixing bowl and rub in the butter until the mixture resembles breadcrumbs. Mix in the egg yolk and sufficient iced water to bind the ingredients. Knead the dough lightly and then chill in the refrigerator for 30 minutes.

4 Sprinkle the cooked bacon pieces over the base of the pastry case and dot with the remaining butter. Pour in the cream and egg mixture. Bake in a preheated oven at 200°C/400°F/Gas Mark 6 for 30 minutes, or until set and golden brown. Serve warm.

PREPARATION: 20 MINUTES +
30 MINUTES CHILLING
COOKING: 30 MINUTES
SERVES: 6

PIPERADE

Hot pepper omelette

3 Beat the eggs together lightly in a bowl. Pour the beaten eggs into a lightly oiled or greased frying pan and cook for 2-3 minutes over very low heat without stirring.

1 Place the red peppers under a preheated hot grill until the skins become charred, turning them frequently. Remove from the heat and place in a polythene bag for a few minutes (this makes it easier to remove the skins). Remove from the bag and skin the peppers. Cut in half and remove the cores and seeds. Slice the flesh thinly.

4 large red peppers
7 tablespoons olive oil
4 large onions, thinly sliced
1 hot pimento, thinly sliced
2 garlic cloves, crushed
pinch of sugar
1kg/2lb tomatoes, skinned, seeded and chopped
1 bouquet garni
salt and freshly ground black pepper
6 thick slices ham, preferably Bayonne
6 eggs

2 Heat 6 tablespoons of oil in a frying pan, add the pepper strips and sauté over medium heat until soft, stirring frequently. Add the onions, pimento and garlic and fry gently for 10 minutes, stirring. Add the sugar, tomatoes, bouquet garni and seasoning. Cook gently for a further 10 minutes, stirring occasionally. Heat the ham gently in a separate pan with the remaining oil.

4 Remove the bouquet garni from the vegetable mixture, then stir into the eggs. Keep stirring until the eggs start to scramble and cook through. Adjust the seasoning to taste. Serve the pipérade straight from the pan accompanied by the slices of ham.

PREPARATION: 15-20 MINUTES
COOKING: 25-30 MINUTES
SERVES: 6

CREPES DE FRUITS DE MER

Seafood pancakes

1 Make the crêpes: sift the flour and salt into a mixing bowl and make a well in the centre. Break in the eggs and add some of the milk. Beat in the flour from the sides of the bowl to make a thick batter. Gradually beat in the remaining milk until the batter is really smooth.

2 Heat a little butter in a small frying pan and pour in sufficient batter to cover the base, tilting the pan. Cook until the underside is golden brown and then flip the crêpe over and cook the other side. Slide out on to a warm plate and make the other crêpes in the same way. Keep warm.

PREPARATION: 20 MINUTES
COOKING: 45 MINUTES
SERVES: 4-6

3 Make the filling: put the monkfish in a saucepan with the wine and poach gently for 10 minutes. Add the scallops and cook for 2-3 minutes. Drain, reserving the liquor. Melt the butter in a small saucepan and fry the onion until golden. Add the mushrooms, fry for 2 minutes and stir in the flour. Cook for 1 minute and add the reserved fish liquor. Bring to the boil and cook for 2 minutes, stirring. Add the cream, fish, scallops, prawns, the seasoning and lemon juice.

125g/4oz flour
pinch of salt
2 eggs
300ml/½ pint milk
butter for frying
4 tablespoons grated Gruyère cheese
For the filling:
250g/8oz monkfish, John Dory or cod, skinned and boned
150ml/¼ pint dry white wine
4 scallops
50g/2oz butter
1 onion, finely chopped
125g/4oz mushrooms, chopped
25g/1oz flour
150ml/¼ pint crème fraîche or double cream
125g/4oz peeled cooked prawns
salt and freshly ground black pepper
1 teaspoon lemon juice

4 Place some of the seafood filling on each crêpe and roll them up. Arrange them in a buttered ovenproof dish and sprinkle the grated cheese over the top. Bake in a preheated oven at 200°C/400°F/Gas Mark 6 for 8-10 minutes until golden brown.

GOUGERE
Savoury choux ring

75g/3oz butter
240ml/7½ fl oz water
125g/4oz plain flour
3 medium eggs, beaten
75g/3oz grated Gruyère cheese
salt and pepper
pinch of cayenne pepper
50g/2oz Gruyère cheese, cut into small dice

1 Sieve the flour at least twice. This is very important if you are to be successful. If there is the slightest lump, you will not lose it in the choux pastry mixture. Put the butter and water in a medium-sized pan and bring to a full, rolling boil.

2 Immediately tip all the flour at once into the pan. Remove from the heat and beat well with a wooden spoon until it forms a ball and leaves the sides of the pan clean. Allow to cool for a few minutes.

3 Gradually add the beaten eggs, a little at a time, beating well between each addition. Beat in 50g/2oz of the grated Gruyère cheese and then add the salt, pepper and cayenne. Lastly, gently fold in the diced Gruyère cheese.

4 Drop tablespoonfuls of the mixture in a circle but not quite touching, on a greased baking sheet. Sprinkle with the remaining grated cheese and then bake in a preheated oven at 220°C/ 425°F/Gas Mark 7 for 25–30 minutes, until well-risen, crisp and golden brown. Cool for a few minutes before serving.

PREPARATION: 15 MINUTES
COOKING: 25–30 MINUTES
SERVES: 4

BOURRIDE

Fish stew

2 Put the pieces of fish and the potatoes into the strained court bouillon. Cover the pan and bring to the boil. Reduce the heat and simmer gently for 15 minutes, or until the fish and potatoes are cooked. Remove with a slotted spoon and transfer to a deep dish or tureen.

1 Make the court bouillon: put the water, white wine, onion, leek, lemon, herbs, fish trimmings, salt and peppercorns into a large saucepan. Bring to the boil and then simmer for 45 minutes. Strain the court bouillon into a clean saucepan.

3 Measure the court bouillon and, if it is necessary, make up to 600ml/1 pint with water. Beat the egg yolks into 150ml/¼ pint of the aioli. Add a little of the court bouillon and blend well together.

1kg/2lb firm white fish, trimmed and cut into large pieces
450g/1lb firm potatoes, peeled and thickly sliced
2 egg yolks
300ml/½ pint aioli (see page 110)
6-8 slices French bread, toasted or fried
2 tablespoons chopped fresh parsley
For the court bouillon:
600ml/1 pint water
150ml/¼ pint dry white wine
1 onion, sliced
1 leek, trimmed and sliced
1 slice of lemon
1 sprig of parsley
1 sprig of thyme
1 sprig of fennel
375g/12oz fish trimmings
1 teaspoon salt
6 black peppercorns

4 Return to the pan with the rest of the court bouillon and cook gently over low heat, stirring all the time, until the sauce is thick enough to coat the back of a spoon. Pour the sauce over the fish and potatoes. To serve, place 1-2 slices of French bread in each hot soup plate. Arrange some fish and potatoes in their sauce on top. Sprinkle with chopped parsley and serve the remaining aioli separately.

PREPARATION: 30 MINUTES
COOKING: 1¼-1½ HOURS
SERVES: 4-6

QUENELLES AVEC CREVETTES

Quenelles in prawn sauce

300g/10oz white fish fillets, e.g. cod, flounder, whiting, pike etc.

salt and freshly ground black pepper

good pinch of ground nutmeg

125ml/4 fl oz double cream

1 egg plus 1 egg white

sprigs of fresh dill

For the sauce:

250g/8oz prawns in their shells

400ml/14 fl oz water

25g/1oz/2 tablespoons butter

2 tablespoons flour

1 tablespoon tomato paste

1/2 teaspoon sugar

100ml/3 1/2 fl oz single cream

50ml/2 fl oz Madeira

salt and pepper

2 Meanwhile make the sauce: peel the prawns, cut into small pieces and set aside. Place the shells in a small saucepan with the water. Cover and simmer for 25–30 minutes. Liquidize the shells and liquid, and push them through a sieve.

1 Cut the fish fillets into pieces, discarding any skin and bones. Process to a smooth purée in a food processor or blender. Add the seasoning, nutmeg, cream, egg and egg white, and process for about 30 seconds until thick and creamy. Chill in the refrigerator for at least 1 hour.

PREPARATION: 10 MINUTES +
1 HOUR CHILLING
COOKING: 1 HOUR
SERVES: 4

3 Heat the butter in a clean small saucepan and stir in the flour. Cook gently for 2 minutes without browning. Add the sieved shell liquid and stir over a low heat until you have a smooth sauce. Simmer gently for 12–14 minutes and then add the tomato paste, sugar and cream. Simmer gently for 5 minutes, add the Madeira and seasoning. Stir in the reserved prawns.

4 Bring a large saucepan of salted water to the boil and then reduce the heat to a simmer. Slide tablespoons of the quenelle mixture into the simmering water. Cook gently for about 5 minutes until set and cooked. Remove with a slotted spoon and keep warm while you cook the rest. Serve the quenelles in a pool of prawn sauce garnished with sprigs of dill.

FILETS DE SOLE A LA NORMANDE

Normandy-style sole

4 sole, about 300g/11oz each, filleted
1 onion, thinly sliced
2 carrots, thinly sliced
1 bouquet garni
400ml/14 fl oz water
300ml/½ pint dry white wine
salt and freshly ground black pepper
150g/5oz butter
125g/4oz button mushrooms
1 tablespoon lemon juice
1.2 litres/2 pints fresh mussels
4 shallots, finely chopped
2 egg yolks
200ml/⅓ pint double cream
125g/4oz shelled cooked prawns
2 tablespoons chopped fresh parsley

2 Season the sole fillets with salt and pepper. Melt 25g/1oz of the butter in a flameproof casserole, add the sole fillets and mushrooms, sprinkle with lemon juice and strain the fish stock over the top. Cover and bake in a preheated oven at 180°C/350°F/Gas Mark 4 for 12-15 minutes, until tender. Remove the sole and mushrooms and keep warm. Reserve the stock.

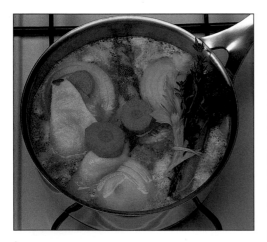

1 Make the fish stock: put any skin and bones (and fish heads if available) from the sole in a large saucepan with the onion, carrot, bouquet garni, water and 200ml/⅓ pint of the white wine. Bring to the boil, then reduce the heat, cover and simmer for 20 minutes.

PREPARATION: 15 MINUTES
COOKING: 1 HOUR
SERVES: 6

3 Wash and scrub the mussels and discard any that are open or cracked. Put them in a large saucepan with the shallots and the remaining wine. Cook over high heat until the shells open, shaking the pan. Discard any that do not open. Remove half of the mussels from their shells. Keep all the mussels warm.

4 Strain the cooking juices from the mussels and sole into a pan and boil steadily until reduced by three-quarters. Remove from the heat. Mix together the egg yolks and cream and stir into the cooking juices. Stir constantly over low heat for 3-4 minutes, without boiling. Whisk in the remaining butter, a little at a time, off the heat and pour the sauce over the sole, shelled mussels and the prawns. Garnish with the mussels in their shells and sprinkle with parsley.

LOUP EN FENOUIL

Charcoal grilled bass with fennel

1 Sprinkle the sea bass with 3 tablespoons of the olive oil and season inside and out with salt and freshly ground black pepper. Stuff the dried fennel stalks inside the fish, and place on a grid over glowing hot charcoal or under a preheated moderate grill. Cook the sea bass for 25–30 minutes, turning the fish over carefully halfway through the cooking.

3 Meanwhile, make the sauce: put the egg yolks in a bowl with the prepared mustard and some salt and freshly ground black pepper. Mix well. Whisk in the oil, a few drops at a time initially and then in a thin steady stream when the sauce starts to emulsify. Whisk vigorously all the time until the sauce thickens.

1 x 1kg/2lb sea bass, cleaned
6 tablespoons olive oil
salt and freshly ground black pepper
few dried fennel stalks
1 large fennel bulb, chopped
2 tablespoons crushed red peppercorns
For the sauce:
2 egg yolks
1 teaspoon prepared French mustard
300ml/$\frac{1}{2}$ pint olive oil
2 tablespoons vinegar
2 gherkins, drained and finely chopped
1 tablespoon drained capers, finely chopped
1 tablespoon chopped fresh parsley
1 tablespoon snipped chives

PREPARATION: 15 MINUTES
COOKING: 25–30 MINUTES
SERVES: 4

2 Heat the remaining olive oil in a small saucepan and add the chopped fennel. Sauté over gentle heat, stirring occasionally, until the fennel is really soft and golden. Season with salt and freshly ground black pepper and keep warm.

4 When the sauce is thick, whisk in the vinegar until thoroughly incorporated. Stir in the gherkins, capers and herbs, and season to taste. Serve the fish, cut into 4 serving pieces, with the sautéed fennel. Sprinkle with crushed red peppercorns and serve the sauce separately.

TRUITES AUX AMANDES

Trout with almonds

4 trout, about 250g/8oz each
200ml/⅓ pint milk
1 tablespoon plain flour
1 tablespoon oil
150g/5oz butter
salt and freshly ground black pepper
125g/4oz flaked almonds
For the garnish:
lemon quarters
2 tablespoons finely chopped parsley

1 Clean and wash the trout under running cold water. Pat dry with absorbent kitchen paper. Put the milk in one dish and the flour in another. Dip each trout into the milk and then coat with flour. Shake gently to remove any excess flour.

2 Heat the oil and 125g/4oz of the butter in a large heavy frying pan. Add the trout and cook gently for about 5 minutes on each side until cooked and golden brown. Take care that the butter does not burn. Remove and place on a warmed serving dish. Sprinkle with salt and pepper and keep the trout warm.

3 Wash out the frying pan and dry thoroughly. Add the remaining butter and heat gently until the butter starts to foam.

4 Add the almonds and cook over moderate heat for about 2 minutes, stirring constantly, until golden all over. Sprinkle the almonds and the butter in the pan over the trout, and serve immediately garnished with lemon quarters and sprinkled with parsley.

PREPARATION: 10 MINUTES
COOKING: 12 MINUTES
SERVES: 4

BOUILLABAISSE

Fish stew from Marseilles

200ml/⅓ pint olive oil
2 onions, thinly sliced
2 leeks, trimmed and thinly sliced
3 tomatoes, skinned, seeded and chopped
4 garlic cloves, crushed
1 sprig of fennel
1 sprig of thyme
1 bay leaf
1 strip orange peel, without pith
750g/1½lb shellfish, e.g. crab, mussels, king prawns
2 litres/3½ pints boiling water
salt and freshly ground black pepper
2.5kg/5lb fish, e.g. John Dory, monkfish, sea bass
4 pinches of saffron powder
To serve:
slices of hot toast
250ml/8 fl oz rouille (see page 110)

2 Add the shellfish, boiling water and some salt and freshly ground black pepper to the pan. Turn up the heat and boil for about 3 minutes to allow the oil and water to amalgamate.

4 When the fish is cooked, taste the bouillabaisse and adjust the seasoning. Stir in the powdered saffron and then pour into a warmed tureen or soup dishes. Serve immediately with slices of hot toast topped with a spoonful of rouille.

3 Add whatever fish you are using to the saucepan and reduce the heat. Continue cooking over medium heat for 12-15 minutes until cooked. The fish should be opaque and tender but still firm - it should not be falling apart.

1 Heat the olive oil in a large saucepan, add the onions, leeks, chopped tomatoes and garlic, and sauté over low heat for a few minutes until soft, stirring frequently. Stir in the fennel, thyme, bay leaf and orange peel.

PREPARATION: 20 MINUTES
COOKING: 30 MINUTES
SERVES: 6-8

MOULES MARINIERE

Sailor-style mussels

1 Put the mussels in a large bowl, cover with cold water and discard any that are open or cracked or rise to the surface. Scrub the mussels well under running cold water to remove any barnacles. Remove the 'beards' with a knife.

2 Melt the butter in a large saucepan, stir in the shallots and garlic and fry gently until soft. Stir in the wine and then add the bouquet garni and bring to the boil. Boil for 2 minutes, add a pinch of salt and some black pepper to taste, and then add the mussels.

PREPARATION: 10–15 MINUTES
COOKING: 20 MINUTES
SERVES: 4-6

3 Cover the pan and cook over high heat, shaking vigorously from time to time, until the mussel shells open. Remove from the pan with a slotted spoon and set aside. Discard any mussels that do not open.

2 litres/3½ pints fresh mussels
60g/2½ oz butter
4 shallots, finely chopped
1 garlic clove, crushed
350ml/12 fl oz dry white wine
1 bouquet garni
salt and freshly ground black pepper
2 tablespoons chopped parsley

4 Boil the liquid rapidly until reduced by half, then return the mussels to the pan and heat through for 1 minute, shaking the pan constantly. Sprinkle with the parsley and shake the pan again. Pile the mussels up in a deep warmed serving dish or in individual dishes and pour the liquid over the top. Serve immediately with crusty bread.

COQUILLES DE FRUITS DE MER

Grilled seafood shells

1 Wash and scrub the mussels and place them in an ovenproof dish with a little water. Put in a preheated oven at 180°C/350°F/Gas Mark 4 until they open. Remove the mussels from the shells, and separate the white parts and corals of the scallops.

2 Melt half of the butter in a frying pan and sauté the onion, garlic and mushrooms until they are lightly coloured. Mix in the mussels and scallops and heat through gently.

PREPARATION: 30 MINUTES
COOKING: 15 MINUTES
SERVES: 4

3 Butter 4 deep scallop shells and sprinkle in half of the breadcrumbs. Divide the seafood mixture between the shells. Boil up 4 tablespoons of water with the wine and lemon juice until reduced, and spoon over the shells.

600ml/1 pint mussels
175g/6oz queen scallops
50g/2oz butter
1 tablespoon finely chopped onion
1 garlic clove, crushed
50g/2oz mushrooms, sliced
50g/2oz fresh white breadcrumbs
150ml/¼ pint dry white wine
1 tablespoon lemon juice
1 tablespoon chopped parsley
salt and freshly ground black pepper

4 Combine the remaining breadcrumbs with the chopped parsley and seasoning and scatter over the shells. Melt the remaining butter and pour over the top. Place the shells on a baking tray and bake in a preheated oven at 180°C/350°F/Gas Mark 4 for 15 minutes until golden brown.

BOEUF EN DAUBE PROVENCAL

Provençal beef stew

1 Put the cubes of beef in a deep bowl with 1 sliced onion, the carrots, orange peel, bay leaf and peppercorns. Pour the red wine over the top, cover the bowl and leave to marinate in the refrigerator overnight. The following day, remove the meat and vegetables and drain well. Reserve the marinade and vegetables.

3 Return the meat to the pan, together with the wine marinade, including the marinated vegetables, orange peel and bay leaf. Discard the peppercorns. Add the stock, salt and pepper, and bring to the boil.

2 Heat the dripping or lard in a flameproof casserole, add the meat and brown on all sides, stirring occasionally. Remove from the pan with a slotted spoon and keep warm. Add the remaining onion and the garlic to the casserole, and cook gently until golden brown.

1kg/2lb lean chuck or stewing steak, trimmed and cut into cubes
2 large onions, sliced
3 carrots, sliced
1 strip orange peel, without pith
1 bay leaf
4–5 peppercorns
300ml/½ pint red wine
50g/2oz dripping or lard
3 garlic cloves, crushed
300ml/½ pint beef stock
salt and freshly ground black pepper

To garnish:

2 tablespoons finely chopped parsley

PREPARATION: 20 MINUTES +
MARINATING OVERNIGHT
COOKING: 2–2½ HOURS
SERVES: 6

4 Cover the casserole and cook in a preheated oven at 160°C/325°F/ Gas Mark 3 for 2–2½ hours, until tender. Discard the bay leaf, and remove the meat from the casserole and keep warm. Boil the sauce until reduced by half. Return the meat to the casserole or place in another dish and pour the sauce over the top. Sprinkle with parsley and serve.

TOURNEDOS EN CROUTE

Fillet steak in pastry

40g/1½ oz butter

1 tablespoon oil

2 small onions, finely chopped

1 garlic clove, crushed

125g/4oz mushrooms, finely chopped

salt and freshly ground black pepper

pinch of ground nutmeg

4 fillet steaks, about 175g/6oz each, trimmed

250g/8oz fresh or frozen puff pastry

1 egg, beaten

4 slices ham

To garnish:

fresh chervil or parsley sprigs

1 Heat 25g/1oz of the butter and the oil in a frying pan and gently cook the onions and garlic until soft. Add the mushrooms, salt, pepper and nutmeg and stir over a gentle heat until the mushrooms are cooked and the moisture has evaporated. Remove from the pan, divide into 8 portions and leave to cool.

PREPARATION: 30 MINUTES
COOKING: 30–35 MINUTES
SERVES: 4

2 Heat the remaining butter in a clean frying pan, add the fillet steaks and then sear quickly on both sides. Remove from the pan, cool quickly and keep chilled until required.

3 Roll out the pastry on a lightly floured surface and cut into 8 rounds large enough to half cover the steaks. Brush a 2.5cm/1 inch border around the edge of each pastry round with beaten egg. Cut the ham into 8 rounds the same size as the steaks.

4 Place one piece of ham on each of 4 pastry rounds. Cover the ham with a portion of the mushroom mixture, a fillet steak, another portion of mushrooms and another round of ham. Top with a pastry circle. Seal the edges of the pastry between your fingers and then with a fork. Cut any pastry trimmings into leaves and use to decorate the croûtes. Brush with beaten egg and cook in a preheated oven at 220°C/425°F/Gas Mark 7 for 20 minutes, until golden brown. Serve with chervil or parsley sprigs.

BOEUF A LA BOURGUIGNONNE

Burgundy-style beef

1 large onion, thinly sliced
few sprigs of parsley
few sprigs of thyme
1 bay leaf, crushed
1kg/2lb chuck steak or top rump, cut into chunks
2 tablespoons marc or brandy
400ml/14 fl oz red Burgundy wine
2 tablespoons olive oil
50g/2oz butter
150g/5oz lean bacon, roughly chopped
24 small pickling onions, peeled
500g/1lb button mushrooms, halved
25g/1oz plain flour
300ml/½ pint beef stock
1 garlic clove, crushed
1 bouquet garni
salt and freshly ground black pepper

1 Put a few onion slices in a deep bowl with a little parsley, thyme and some crumbled bay leaf. Place a few pieces of beef on top, and continue layering up in this way until all the onion, beef and herbs are used. Mix together the marc or brandy with the wine and oil, and pour over the beef. Cover and leave to marinate for at least 4 hours.

3 Remove the beef from the marinade, then strain the marinade and set aside. Add the beef to the casserole and fry briskly until browned on all sides. Sprinkle in the flour and cook, stirring, for 1 minute. Gradually stir in the strained marinade, then add the stock, garlic and bouquet garni. Season to taste, cover and simmer gently for 2 hours.

2 Melt the butter in a flameproof casserole, add the bacon and fry over moderate heat until golden brown. Remove and set aside. Add the small onions and fry until golden on all sides. Remove and set aside. Add the mushrooms and fry, stirring, for 1 minute. Drain and set aside.

PREPARATION: 30 MINUTES +
4 HOURS MARINATING
COOKING: 2½ HOURS
SERVES: 4–6

4 Skim off any fat on the surface, and add the bacon, onions and mushrooms to the casserole. Cover and simmer for 30 minutes, or until the beef is tender. Discard the bouquet garni and serve immediately.

GIGOT AU PISTOU

Leg of lamb with garlic stuffing

1 x 2kg/4lb leg of lamb
75g/3oz butter
500g/1lb potatoes, peeled and cut into 5mm/¼ inch slices
5 tablespoons olive oil
freshly ground sea salt and black pepper
small sprigs of fresh rosemary
For the pistou:
125g/4oz streaky bacon rashers, chopped
3 garlic cloves, crushed
2 teaspoons finely chopped fresh basil
1 tablespoon finely chopped fresh parsley

1 Make the pistou: mix together the chopped bacon, crushed garlic, chopped fresh basil and parsley in a small bowl.

3 Spread the lamb with 50g/2oz of the butter and place in a roasting pan. Cook in a preheated oven at 180°C/350°F/Gas Mark 4 for 2-2½ hours, according to how pink or well done you like your lamb.

2 Make an incision in the leg of lamb up to the bone and place the pistou mixture inside. Pull the sides of the joint together to enclose the stuffing. Sew it up with a trussing needle and string.

4 Add the potatoes to a pan of boiling salted water and cook for 4-5 minutes. Drain well. Just before the meat is cooked, heat the remaining butter and oil in a frying pan and then sauté the potatoes, turning frequently, until crisp and golden. Season with salt and pepper. Remove the string from the lamb, and serve garnished with small sprigs of rosemary, with the sautéed potatoes. If wished, you can use the meat fat to make some gravy.

PREPARATION: 25 MINUTES
COOKING: 2-2½ HOURS
SERVES: 6

SAUTE DE PORC CATALANE

Catalan pork stew

150ml/¼ pint olive oil
750g/1½lb lean pork, cut into 2.5cm/1 inch cubes
1 large onion, peeled and sliced
2 garlic cloves, crushed
500g/1lb tomatoes, skinned and chopped
1 green pepper, seeded and chopped
1½ teaspoons paprika
150ml/¼ pint chicken stock
salt and freshly ground black pepper
1 aubergine, sliced
2-3 tablespoons seasoned flour
chopped fresh coriander leaves to garnish

2 Add the onion and garlic and cook until soft and golden. Return the meat to the pan, and stir in the tomatoes, green pepper, paprika and stock. Season with salt and freshly ground black pepper. Bring to the boil, cover with greaseproof paper and a lid, and simmer gently for 1 hour, or until the meat is tender.

1 Heat 2 tablespoons of the oil in a large saucepan or flameproof casserole, add the pork and sauté gently until golden brown on all sides, turning occasionally. Remove from the pan with a slotted spoon.

3 Meanwhile, sprinkle the aubergine slices with salt and leave in a colander for at least 30 minutes to exude their bitter juice. Wash the aubergine and pat dry with absorbent kitchen paper.

4 Dip the aubergine slices in seasoned flour. Heat some of the remaining oil in a large frying pan. When it is hot, fry the aubergine slices, a few at a time, until they are golden brown on both sides. Add more oil as required. Remove with a slotted spoon and pat dry with absorbent kitchen paper. Serve the pork with the fried aubergine, scattered with coriander, with plain boiled rice.

PREPARATION: 20 MINUTES
COOKING: 1¼ HOURS
SERVES: 4

PORC AUX PRUNEAUX DE TOURS

Pork Touraine-style

1 Soak the prunes in the white wine for several hours, or preferably leave them overnight. Put the soaked prunes in an ovenproof dish with 300ml/½ pint of the soaking liquid. Cover the dish and cook gently in a preheated oven at 150°C/ 300°F/ Gas Mark 2 for about 1 hour.

3 Add the remaining soaking liquid from the prunes, and the mushrooms to the pan. Cover the pan and cook gently over low heat at a bare simmer for about 30 minutes. Turn the noisettes over halfway through the cooking time.

2 Coat the pork noisettes lightly on both sides with the flour seasoned with salt and black pepper. Heat the butter in a large frying pan and sauté the noisettes until they are lightly browned on both sides.

PREPARATION: SOAKING
OVERNIGHT
COOKING: 1¼ HOURS
SERVES: 4

300g/10oz large prunes
450ml/¾ pint dry white wine
4 pork noisettes
2 tablespoons flour
salt and freshly ground black pepper
50g/2oz butter
150g/5oz button mushrooms
2 tablespoons redcurrant jelly
200ml/7 fl oz crème fraîche
3 tablespoons chopped parsley

4 Remove the noisettes and keep warm with the prunes. Add the remaining liquid in which the prunes were cooked to the pan together with the redcurrant jelly, and boil until the sauce reduces. Reduce the heat to a simmer and gradually stir in the crème fraîche. Heat very gently without boiling and adjust the seasoning. Serve the pork and prunes with the sauce, sprinkled with parsley.

CASSOULET TOULOUSAIN

Traditional stew from Toulouse

500g/1lb dried white haricot beans
375g/12oz belly pork, boned
1 small ham hock
2 carrots, thickly sliced
1 onion, peeled and stuck with 3 cloves
2 tomatoes, skinned and chopped
2 garlic cloves, crushed
1.5 litres/2½ pints water
For the sauté:
3 tablespoons olive oil
375g/12oz boned shoulder of lamb, cubed
2 onions, chopped
2 garlic cloves, crushed
2 tomatoes, skinned and chopped
salt and freshly ground black pepper
bouquet garni
2 Toulouse sausages, thickly sliced
250g/8oz confit d'oie(optional)
75g/3oz dried breadcrumbs

1 Soak the beans in cold water overnight. Rinse and drain them the following day. Soak the belly pork and ham hock overnight to reduce the saltiness. Put the drained beans, pork and ham in a large saucepan with the carrots, onion, tomatoes, garlic and water. Simmer gently for 2 hours, or until tender.

3 Ladle in sufficient cooking liquid from the bean pan to cover the lamb. Add the tomatoes, seasoning and bouquet garni. Cover the pan and simmer gently for 1½ hours. Brown the sausages in a small pan and then add to the lamb for a further 10 minutes.

2 Meanwhile, heat the olive oil in a large frying pan and add the lamb. Sauté until lightly browned on all sides. Add the onions and garlic and sauté until softened and golden.

4 Remove the pork and ham and cut into chunks. Put half the beans in a large ovenproof dish and add the chunks of ham and pork, the confit d'oie (if using) and the lamb mixture with its liquid. Cover with the remaining beans and sprinkle with breadcrumbs. Bake in a preheated oven at 150°C/300°F/Gas Mark 2 for 1 hour.

PREPARATION: 30 MINUTES +
SOAKING OVERNIGHT
COOKING: 3 HOURS
SERVES: 6-8

RIS DE VEAU A LA NORMANDE

Sweetbreads with mushrooms and cream

1 Soak the sweetbreads in a bowl of cold water for 3 hours, changing the water 2 or 3 times. Drain the sweetbreads and rinse thoroughly under running cold water. Put them in a saucepan, cover with fresh water and bring slowly to the boil. Simmer for 5 minutes, then drain and rinse again under running cold water.

2 Remove any fatty bits and then place the sweetbreads between 2 plates. Weight them down and leave for 1 hour. Melt half of the butter in a frying pan. Slice the sweetbreads and add to the pan. Fry gently until they are lightly coloured on both sides.

3 Coat the mushrooms with the flour, shaking off any excess, and add them to the pan. Season with salt and pepper, then cover and simmer very gently for 15 minutes. Remove the sweetbreads and mushrooms with a slotted spoon and keep warm.

4 calf's sweetbreads
150g/5oz butter
250g/8oz mushrooms, sliced
2 tablespoons plain flour
salt and freshly ground black pepper
7 tablespoons calvados or brandy
200ml/⅓ pint double cream
1 tablespoon chopped fresh parsley

PREPARATION: 10 MINUTES +
4 HOURS SOAKING
COOKING: 30 MINUTES
SERVES: 4-6

4 Stir the calvados or brandy into the pan and scrape up the sediment from the bottom. Stir in the cream and simmer over very low heat until reduced by half. Remove from the heat and whisk in the remaining butter, a little at a time. Pour over the sweetbreads and mushrooms and serve sprinkled with parsley.

ROGNONS A LA BOURGUIGNONNE

Lamb's kidneys in Burgundy

25g/1oz butter
1 tablespoon olive oil
1 onion, finely chopped
125g/4oz mushrooms, chopped
125g/4oz unsmoked bacon, diced
8 lamb's kidneys
300ml/½ pint Burgundy or other dry red wine
salt and freshly ground black pepper
1 garlic clove, crushed
bouquet garni
1 tablespoon flour
1 tablespoon chopped fresh parsley

2 Remove the membrane surrounding the kidneys and trim away the fat. Split the kidneys in half lengthways and, using a sharp knife, remove the central white cores. Add the prepared kidneys to the pan and cook them over high heat to seal them. Reduce the heat and cook gently for 3-4 minutes. Remove from the pan and keep warm.

1 Heat half of the butter and the oil in a heavy frying pan. Add the onion, mushrooms and bacon, and sauté gently until golden. Remove them from the pan with a slotted spoon and keep warm.

3 Add the red wine to the frying pan together with the onion, mushroom and bacon mixture. Season with salt and pepper, and stir in the garlic and bouquet garni. Simmer gently for 10 minutes.

4 Mix the remaining butter with the flour to make a *beurre manié*, and add to the sauce, a little at a time, stirring all the time until it thickens. Pour the sauce over the kidneys and serve sprinkled with parsley.

PREPARATION: 15 MINUTES
COOKING: 25 MINUTES
SERVES: 4

COQ AU VIN

Chicken in red wine

2 tablespoons oil
50g/2oz butter
1 x 2.5kg/5lb chicken, cut into 12 serving pieces
24 small pickling onions, peeled
125g/4oz diced smoked bacon
1 tablespoon plain flour
1 bottle good red wine, e.g. Burgundy
1 bouquet garni
2 garlic cloves
pinch of sugar
freshly grated nutmeg
salt and freshly ground black pepper
24 button mushrooms
1 tablespoon brandy
3-4 slices bread
oil for frying
2 tablespoons chopped parsley

3 Add the mushrooms and continue cooking gently for a further 45 minutes, or until the chicken is cooked and tender. Remove the chicken with a slotted spoon and arrange the pieces on a warm serving platter. Keep hot. Pour the brandy into the sauce and boil, uncovered, for 5 minutes until thick and reduced. Remove the bouquet garni and garlic cloves.

1 Heat the oil and butter in a large flameproof casserole and add the chicken pieces. Fry gently over low heat until golden on all sides, turning occasionally. Remove with a slotted spoon and keep warm. Pour off a little of the fat from the casserole, then add the onions and bacon. Sauté until lightly coloured, then sprinkle in the flour and stir well.

PREPARATION: 15-20 MINUTES
COOKING: 1½ HOURS
SERVES: 6-8

2 Pour in the wine and bring to the boil, stirring. Add the bouquet garni, unpeeled garlic cloves, sugar and nutmeg, and salt and pepper to taste. Return the chicken to the casserole, lower the heat, cover and simmer for 15 minutes.

4 Remove the crusts from the bread and cut into pieces. Fry in oil until crisp and golden on both sides. Remove and pat with absorbent kitchen paper. Pour the sauce over the chicken and serve with the bread croûtes. Sprinkle with chopped parsley.

POULET BASQUAISE

Basque-style chicken

1 Heat the olive oil in a sauté pan or deep frying pan. Add the diced ham or bacon and sauté gently, stirring occasionally, until lightly browned. Remove the ham from the pan with a slotted spoon and keep warm.

3 Add the tomatoes and some stock (300ml/$^1/_2$ pint for fresh tomatoes; 150ml/$^1/_4$ pint for canned tomatoes in juice). Season with salt and pepper. Return the chicken and ham to the pan, cover and cook gently for 40–45 minutes, or until the chicken is cooked and tender.

2 Add the chicken portions to the pan and cook, turning occasionally, until they are uniformly brown all over. Remove with a slotted spoon and keep warm. Add the onions and garlic to the pan and cook gently until soft and golden. Add the peppers and marjoram, cover and cook gently for 10 minutes.

4 tablespoons olive oil
175g/6oz smoked ham or streaky bacon, diced
4 large chicken portions
4 onions, sliced
3 garlic cloves, crushed
2 green peppers, seeded and diced
$^1/_4$ teaspoon dried marjoram
425g/14oz fresh or canned tomatoes
150–300ml/$^1/_4$–$^1/_2$ pint chicken stock
salt and freshly ground black pepper
2 tablespoons chopped fresh parsley

4 Remove the chicken and transfer to a serving dish. Boil the sauce gently to reduce it if necessary, until it is thick enough to coat the back of a spoon. Adjust the seasoning and pour over the chicken. Sprinkle with chopped parsley and serve.

PREPARATION: 20 MINUTES
COOKING: 1 HOUR
SERVES: 4

CANARD A L'ORANGE

Duck with oranges

25g/1oz butter

3 tablespoons olive oil

1 x 2kg/4lb duck, trussed with thread or string

4 garlic cloves, crushed

125g/4oz raw country ham, cut into thin strips

600ml/1 pint dry white wine

200ml/7 fl oz chicken stock

1 bouquet garni

salt and freshly ground black pepper

pared rind and juice of 2 oranges

1 tablespoon wine vinegar

2 oranges, cut into thin rings

For the beurre manié:

1 tablespoon flour

25g/1oz butter, softened

2 Add the garlic and strips of ham to the casserole and fry for 1-2 minutes. Pour in the white wine and stock, bring to the boil and them simmer for a few minutes until slightly reduced. Add the bouquet garni, salt and pepper and orange juice, and then cover the casserole. Reduce the heat and simmer gently for 1½ hours, or until the duck is cooked. Baste occasionally during cooking.

1 Heat the butter and oil in a deep flameproof casserole and add the duck. Fry over medium heat, turning the duck as necesssary, until it is golden brown all over.

PREPARATION: 20 MINUTES
COOKING: 1½ HOURS
SERVES: 6

3 Using a sharp knife, cut the pared orange rind into fine strips, and plunge them into a small pan of boiling water. Blanch for 5 minutes, then remove and drain. Dry thoroughly on absorbent kitchen paper and set aside.

4 Make the *beurre manié:* blend the flour and butter. Remove the cooked duck from the casserole, cut into serving pieces and keep warm. Boil the cooking liquid for about 10 minutes, until reduced. Add the vinegar, strips of orange rind and little pieces of *beurre manié,* stirring all the time, until the sauce thickens. Carve the duck and serve with the orange sauce, garnished with orange rings.

SALADE DE LENTILLES TIEDE

Warm lentil salad

1 Put the lentils in a bowl, cover with water and leave to soak for 3-4 hours. Drain well and put them in a large saucepan.

3 Slice the remaining carrot thinly and blanch in a saucepan of lightly salted boiling water with the leek and celery. Drain well.

2 Peel one of the carrots and add to the lentils in the saucepan together with the onion studded with the clove, the bay leaf, thyme and garlic. Cover with cold water and bring to the boil, then simmer for 30-35 minutes. Remove and discard the vegetables, bay leaf and garlic, and drain the lentils.

375g/12oz green lentils, soaked in water for 3-4 hours
2 carrots
1 onion, peeled
1 clove
1 bay leaf
pinch of dried thyme
1 garlic clove, peeled
1 leek, thinly sliced
125g/4oz celery, chopped
200g/7oz smoked streaky bacon, diced
1 tablespoon oil
1 tablespoon snipped chives
For the vinaigrette:
200ml/⅓ pint walnut oil
6 tablespoons sherry or wine vinegar
1 tablespoon Dijon mustard
salt and pepper

4 Meanwhile, whisk the ingredients together for the vinaigrette dressing, and fry the bacon in the oil until crisp. Stir the blanched vegetables and fried bacon gently into the lentils and toss in the vinaigrette dressing. Sprinkle with snipped chives and serve warm.

PREPARATION: 10 MINUTES + 3-4 HOURS SOAKING
COOKING: 45 MINUTES
SERVES: 4

SALADE NICOISE

Tuna salad from Nice

1 Rub around the inside of a large salad bowl with the bruised garlic clove. Line the bowl with lettuce leaves. Chop the remaining lettuce leaves roughly and then arrange them in the bottom of the bowl.

2 Mix together the celery and cucumber with the French beans and artichoke hearts. Arrange on top of the lettuce in the salad bowl.

1 garlic clove, peeled and bruised
1 lettuce
125g/4oz celery hearts, thinly sliced
125g/4oz cucumber, peeled and thinly sliced
250g/8oz small French beans, topped and tailed
250g/8oz canned artichoke hearts, thinly sliced
500g/1lb tomatoes, skinned, seeded and quartered
1 large green pepper, seeded and sliced
1 onion, sliced
4 hard-boiled eggs, halved
50g/2oz black olives
8 canned anchovy fillets, drained
1 x 250g/8oz can tuna fish in oil, drained

For the dressing:
7 tablespoons olive oil
4 basil leaves, finely chopped
salt and freshly ground black pepper

PREPARATION: 20 MINUTES
SERVES: 4

3 Arrange the quartered tomatoes, sliced pepper and onion, eggs, olives and anchovies on top of the mixed vegetables in the bowl. Cut the tuna into chunks and place in the bowl.

4 Make the dressing: mix together the olive oil and chopped basil with the seasoning. Pour the dressing over the salad and transfer to individual serving plates.

RATATOUILLE NICOISE

Vegetable stew from Nice

1 Make a small incision in each tomato with a sharp knife. Put them in a bowl and cover with boiling water. Leave for 1-2 minutes, then remove and skin the tomatoes. Chop them roughly.

3 Add the courgettes and continue frying for 5-6 minutes until they are lightly coloured. Remove the aubergines and courgettes from the pan with a slotted spoon, and set aside.

750g/1½lb tomatoes
125ml/4 fl oz olive oil
500g/1lb aubergines, thinly sliced or diced
500g/1lb courgettes, sliced
500g/1lb onions, thinly sliced
500g/1lb green peppers, seeded and thinly sliced
5 garlic cloves, crushed
salt and freshly ground black pepper
2 sprigs of thyme
5 basil leaves
To garnish:
chopped parsley

PREPARATION: 30 MINUTES
COOKING: 40 MINUTES
SERVES: 6

2 Heat half of the oil in a large heavy saucepan and add the aubergines. Fry them gently over moderate heat until they are lightly golden, stirring frequently.

4 Add the remaining oil to the pan. Stir in the onions and fry gently until soft and golden. Add the peppers and garlic, increase the heat and fry for 3-4 minutes. Add the tomatoes and cook gently for 10 minutes. Stir in the aubergines and courgettes, season to taste and crumble in the thyme. Cook gently, uncovered, for about 40 minutes. Crumble the basil leaves into the ratatouille, and serve it warm or cold, sprinkled with parsley.

GALETTES DE POMMES DE TERRE
Potato cakes

1 Peel the potatoes and grate them coarsely with a grater or in a food processor. Put the grated potatoes in a sieve and rinse well under running cold water. Drain and transfer the potatoes to a bowl.

2 Break the eggs into the bowl of grated potatoes and mix together. Add the chopped onions, flour, herbs and garlic. Season with salt and pepper and a little grated nutmeg, and stir the mixture thoroughly.

3 Divide the potato mixture into equal-sized portions and mould them into small cakes, using a spoon to shape them.

1kg/2lb potatoes
3 eggs
125g/4oz onions, chopped
1 tablespoon flour
1 tablespoon chopped parsley and chives
1 garlic clove, crushed
salt and pepper
freshly grated nutmeg
6 tablespoons oil

4 Heat the oil in a frying pan. When it is hot, add the potato cakes and fry until golden brown and crisp on both sides, turning them once during cooking. Serve them very hot with a meat dish, or with some charcuterie and a green salad.

PREPARATION: 20 MINUTES
COOKING: 5-10 MINUTES
SERVES: 4

GRATIN D'ASPERGES AU JAMBON

Asparagus and ham au gratin

1 Cook the asparagus for 15–20 minutes in boiling salted water to which the lemon juice and sugar have been added. The asparagus should be tender but still firm. Leave to cool in the cooking liquid.

2 Put the cream and stock in a small saucepan and boil until reduced by half. Season to taste with salt and pepper and a little grated nutmeg. Remove the pan from the heat.

3 Drain the asparagus carefully so as not to damage the delicate spears. Divide them into 4 equal-sized bundles and roll each one in a slice of ham. Arrange the ham bundles in a buttered ovenproof dish.

4 Pour the reduced cream mixture over the top and sprinkle with the grated cheese. Bake in a preheated oven at 200°C/400°F/Gas Mark 6 for 20–25 minutes until bubbling and golden brown. Serve immediately.

375g/12oz thin asparagus, trimmed
salt
juice of 1 lemon
1 teaspoon sugar
300ml/½ pint single cream
200ml/⅓ pint chicken stock
salt and pepper
freshly grated nutmeg
4 slices boiled ham
15g/½oz butter
125g/4oz grated cheese

PREPARATION: 20–25 MINUTES
COOKING: 20–25 MINUTES
SERVES: 4

FARCIS PROVENCAUX

Provençal stuffed vegetables

1 Cut the aubergines in half lengthways, scoop out the flesh and reserve. Plunge the onions into boiling water for a few minutes, drain and hollow out the centres, reserving the scooped-out flesh. Cut a hole in the top of each tomato, scoop out the flesh and reserve. Sprinkle some salt, pepper and a little of the olive oil inside the hollow vegetables.

2 Prepare the stuffing: mix together in a bowl the veal or pork, onion, garlic, parsley and the reserved flesh from the hollowed-out vegetables.

3 Heat 1 tablespoon of olive oil in a frying pan and add the stuffing mixture. Fry gently for 4-5 minutes, stirring constantly. Remove the pan from the heat and then stir in the Parmesan cheese, rice and crumbled thyme. Stir in the beaten egg and season to taste with salt and pepper.

4 Put the hollowed-out vegetables on 2 large baking trays and divide the stuffing between them. Sprinkle with olive oil. Bake in a preheated oven at 180°C/350°F/Gas Mark 4 for 45 minutes, sprinkling with more oil as necessary.

3 aubergines
6 large onions
6 large tomatoes
salt and freshly ground black pepper
7 tablespoons olive oil

For the stuffing:

375g/12oz minced veal or pork
1 onion, finely chopped
2 garlic cloves, crushed
few parsley sprigs, chopped
2 tablespoons grated Parmesan cheese
2 tablespoons boiled long-grain rice
2 sprigs of thyme, crumbled
2 eggs, beaten

PREPARATION: 30 MINUTES
COOKING: 45 MINUTES
SERVES: 6

GRATIN DAUPHINOIS

Layered creamy potatoes

1 garlic clove, peeled
75g/3oz softened butter
1kg/2lb waxy potatoes
salt and freshly ground black pepper
freshly grated nutmeg
350ml/12 fl oz hot milk
250ml/8 fl oz single cream

1 Cut the garlic clove and use it to rub round the inside of a large earthenware baking dish to exude its flavour and aroma to the finished dish. Brush the dish thickly with some of the softened butter.

2 Peel the potatoes and slice into thin rounds. Arrange a layer in the bottom of the prepared dish and sprinkle with salt, pepper and grated nutmeg. Continue layering up the potatoes in this way, seasoning each layer, until they are all used.

3 Mix the hot milk and cream together, and then pour the mixture over the layered potatoes, making sure that the potatoes are almost totally covered by the liquid.

4 Dot the top with the remaining butter and bake in a preheated oven at 180°C/350°F/Gas Mark 4 for 1-1¼ hours, or until the potatoes are tender when pierced with a skewer. Increase the oven temperature to 200°C/400°F/Gas Mark 6 for the last 10 minutes of cooking time to brown the top layer of potatoes. Serve hot, straight from the baking dish.

PREPARATION: 15-20 MINUTES
COOKING: 1-1¼ HOURS
SERVES: 4-6

TIAN
Provençal baked vegetables

1 Put the aubergine slices in a colander and sprinkle with salt. Leave for 30 minutes to exude their bitter juices. Rinse well under running cold water and pat dry.

2 Sauté the sliced aubergine with the onions, peppers and garlic in 4 tablespoons of the olive oil until golden. Spread the mixture over the base of a shallow oval ovenproof dish.

1 aubergine sliced
salt
2 onions, thinly sliced
2 red peppers, seeded and sliced
4 garlic cloves, crushed
6 tablespoons olive oil
freshly ground black pepper
2 large courgettes
3 large tomatoes
sprigs of fresh thyme and rosemary
3 tablespoons fresh white breadcrumbs
2 tablespoons grated Parmesan cheese

4 Remove the dish from the oven and sprinkle with the breadcrumbs and Parmesan. Drizzle a little more olive oil over the top if wished. Bake for a further 10 minutes until crisp and golden. Eat hot, warm or cold.

3 Remove some of the peel in strips from the sides of the courgettes with a potato peeler, leaving some vertical stripes of green. Slice the courgettes thinly. Slice the tomatoes. Arrange the courgette and tomato slices in alternate rows over the top of the sautéed vegetable mixture, overlapping them like fish scales. Season to taste with some salt and pepper and add a few sprigs of thyme and rosemary. Bake in a preheated oven at 190°C/375°F/Gas Mark 5 for 25 minutes until golden.

PREPARATION: 45 MINUTES
COOKING: 25 MINUTES
SERVES: 4

OEUFS A LA NEIGE AU CITRON

Lemon snow eggs

1 Put the egg whites in a large clean bowl and whisk well until they form firm peaks. Gradually whisk in 125g/4oz of the sugar. Fold in the grated lemon zest.

2 Beat the egg yolks together and add 2 tablespoons of the cold milk. Bring the rest of the milk to the boil in a large saucepan, add the lemon peel and stir in the remaining sugar. Reduce the heat.

3 Drop teaspoons of the beaten egg white into the hot milk and poach gently for 2 minutes. Remove with a slotted spoon, drain on absorbent kitchen paper and set aside while you make the lemon custard.

5 eggs, separated
finely grated zest of ½ lemon
600ml/1 pint milk
strip of lemon peel
175g/6oz caster sugar

4 Cool the milk and stir in the beaten egg yolks. Heat the mixture gently in a double boiler, or a basin, over simmering water, stirring continuously until the custard thickens. Do not allow to boil. Remove the lemon peel and let the custard cool down. Pour into a shallow serving dish and float the meringues on top. Chill well before serving.

PREPARATION: 15–20 MINUTES
COOKING: 20–30 MINUTES
SERVES: 4

TARTE AUX POMMES ALSACIENNE

Alsace-style apple tart

25g/1oz butter
250g/8oz pâte brisée(see page 110)
1kg/2lb green dessert apples
150g/5oz caster sugar
1 teaspoon ground cinnamon
3 tablespoons milk
150ml/¼ pint single cream
2 eggs
25g/1oz icing sugar

1 Butter a 25cm/10 inch loose-bottomed flan tin and line with the pâte brisée (shortcrust pastry). Prick the base of the pastry case all over with a fork.

2 Peel, core and quarter the apples. Slice the quartered apples without separating the slices and spread them out fan-fashion on the base of the tart in an attractive pattern.

3 Sprinkle the apples with 25g/1oz of the sugar and then with the ground cinnamon. Bake in a preheated oven at 200°C/400°F/Gas Mark 6 for 20 minutes.

4 Mix the remaining sugar in a bowl with the milk, cream and eggs. Beat lightly and then pour over the cooked apples. Return to the oven for a further 10-15 minutes. When the tart is cooked and the custard set, dust with icing sugar and serve warm.

PREPARATION: 20 MINUTES
COOKING: 30-35 MINUTES
SERVES: 6-8

CREPES SUZETTE

Sweet orange pancakes

125g/4oz plain flour

¼ teaspoon salt

3 eggs

2 tablespoons oil

50g/2oz melted butter

1 tablespoon caster sugar

2 teaspoons vanilla sugar

350ml/12 fl oz milk

25g/1oz butter for frying

For the syrup:

125g/4oz softened butter, diced

125g/4oz caster sugar

grated rind and juice of 1 orange

6 tablespoons Cointreau or Grand Marnier

3 tablespoons brandy

2 Melt a little of the butter in a small frying pan and when it is really hot, ladle some of the batter into the pan. Tilt the pan so that the batter covers the base evenly and fry until golden brown on the underside. Flip the crêpe over and cook the other side. Slide onto a warm plate and keep warm while you cook the other crêpes.

3 Make the syrup: put the butter and sugar in a bowl and beat together until smooth and creamy. Beat the orange rind and juice into the creamed mixture, and then beat in 3 tablespoons of the orange liqueur and 1 tablespoon of the brandy.

4 Transfer the orange mixture to a large frying pan and heat gently. Boil rapidly for 1-2 minutes, and reduce the heat. Add the crêpes, one at a time, folding each one in half and then in half again. Simmer gently until hot. Warm the remaining liqueur and brandy in a small pan, set alight and pour flaming over the crêpes just before serving, or cook and set alight at the table.

1 Make the batter: sift the flour and salt into a bowl and make a well in the centre. Tip in the eggs, oil, melted butter, sugar and milk, and beat until smooth, using a hand-held electric whisk if wished.

PREPARATION: 25 MINUTES
COOKING: 6-8 MINUTES
SERVES: 6-8

TARTE AU FROMAGE BLANC

Cheesecake

1 Put the raisins in a small bowl with the Kirsch. Leave to soak while you prepare the cheesecake. Line a 23cm/9 inch loose-bottomed flan tin with the pâte brisée (shortcrust pastry). Prick the base with a fork.

3 Pour the cream cheese filling into the shortcrust pastry case. Sprinkle the surface of the tart with the soaked raisins. Place in a preheated oven at 180°C/350°F/Gas Mark 4.

2 Put the fromage blanc in a bowl and mix in the cream and sugar. Gently beat in the egg yolks, arrowroot and lemon rind. Beat the egg whites until stiff and fold gently into the cream cheese mixture.

PREPARATION: 20 MINUTES
COOKING: 50 MINUTES
SERVES: 6

25g/1oz raisins
1 tablespoon Kirsch
250g/8oz pâte brisée (see page 110)
200g/7oz fromage blanc
3 tablespoons single cream
125g/4oz sugar
3 eggs, separated
15g/½oz arrowroot
grated rind of 1 lemon
icing sugar for dusting

4 After 10 minutes, lower the oven temperature to 150°C/300°F/Gas Mark 2, and bake for a further 40 minutes. The cheesecake is cooked when the blade of a knife inserted into it comes out dry. Remove from the tin and cool. When cold, dust with icing sugar, and then serve.

CREME CARAMEL

Caramel custard

500ml/17 fl oz milk
1 vanilla pod, split in half lengthways
4 eggs
50g/2oz sugar
For the caramel:
50g/2oz sugar
1 tablespoon water
1 teaspoon lemon juice

1 Put the milk and vanilla pod in a heavy saucepan and bring to the boil. Remove from the heat and leave for 5 minutes to infuse. Whisk the eggs and sugar together in a bowl until thoroughly combined. Discard the vanilla and whisk the milk into the egg and sugar mixture.

3 Pour the caramel into 6 small moulds or 1 large 1 litre/1³/₄ pint charlotte mould. Rotate the moulds quickly so that the caramel coats the base and sides evenly.

4 Strain the custard through a fine sieve. Pour into the moulds and stand in a roasting pan half-filled with water (*bain marie*). Cook in a preheated oven at 150°C/300°F/Gas Mark 2 for about 45 minutes, or until set. Leave to cool and then chill in the refrigerator before unmoulding. To unmould, dip the base of the moulds into a bowl of hot water for 30 seconds and then turn out on to a serving plate.

2 While the milk is infusing, make the caramel. Put the sugar, water and lemon juice in a small saucepan and cook over moderate heat, stirring well until the sugar dissolves. When it turns a rich golden caramel colour, remove from the heat immediately.

PREPARATION: 15 MINUTES
COOKING: 45 MINUTES
SERVES: 4–5

TARTE TATIN

Upside-down apple tart

1 Make the caramel: put the sugar and water in a flameproof oval or round baking dish and place over low heat. Stir well to dissolve the sugar completely, then turn up the heat and cook until the sugar starts to caramelize and go golden brown. Remove quickly from the heat and stir in the butter. Add a little hot water if necessary to thin the caramel, standing well back.

1.5gk/3lb crisp dessert apples, e.g. Granny Smiths
75g/3oz caster sugar
75g/3oz butter
250g/8oz fresh or frozen puff pastry
For the caramel:
75g/3oz caster sugar
3 tablespoons water
25g/1oz butter

2 Peel and core the apples. Cut each one in half and pack tightly into the dish, arranging them in concentric circles so that each round side fits neatly into a hollowed-out side.

3 Sprinkle the apples with the caster sugar. Cut the butter into small dice and scatter across the top of the apples. Cook in the preheated oven at 190°C/375°F/Gas Mark 5 for about 20 minutes.

4 Roll out the puff pastry on a lightly floured board and place on top of the apples. Tuck in the pastry edges around the side of the dish. Increase the oven temperature to 220°C/425°F/Gas Mark 7 and bake for a further 15–20 minutes until the pastry is well-risen and golden brown. Cool a little and then invert the tart on to a serving platter. Serve warm with cream or crème fraîche.

PREPARATION: 20 MINUTES
COOKING: 35–40 MINUTES
SERVES: 6

PARIS-BREST

Choux ring with praline cream filling

50g/2oz butter

150ml/¼ pint water

pinch of salt

65g/2½oz plain flour, sifted

2 large eggs

25g/1oz flaked almonds

icing sugar for dusting

For the praline cream:

75g/3oz blanched almonds

75g/3oz caster sugar

300ml/½ pint double cream, whipped

2 Beat in the eggs, one at a time, and then put the choux paste in a piping bag fitted with a 1cm/½ inch plain nozzle. Pipe a ring, 20cm/8 inches in diameter, on to a greased baking sheet, then another ring inside the first one, and a ring on top. Sprinkle with almonds and bake in a preheated oven at 200°C/400°F/Gas Mark 6 for 30 minutes or until well risen and golden brown. Cool on a wire rack.

1 Make the choux pastry: put the butter, water and salt in a medium-sized saucepan and bring to the boil. Tip in the sifted flour all at once and remove from the heat. Beat with a wooden spoon until the choux paste is smooth and leaves the sides of the pan clean.

4 Pour the mixture on to an oiled baking sheet, and set aside until cold and crisp. Grind to a fine powder in a food processor or electric grinder, and mix into the whipped cream. Split the choux ring horizontally, and fill with the praline cream. Place the top in position and serve the choux ring dusted with icing sugar.

3 Make the praline: put the blanched almonds and sugar in a small heavy-bottomed saucepan, and stir over gentle heat until the sugar melts and caramelizes and the almonds are toasted.

PREPARATION: 30 MINUTES
COOKING: 30 MINUTES
SERVES: 6

TARTE CITRON

Lemon tart

1 Make the pastry: sift the flour and salt into a bowl and rub in the butter until the mixture resembles breadcrumbs. Stir in the egg yolk and sufficient iced water to make a soft and pliable dough. Chill in the refrigerator for 30 minutes

3 Roll out the pastry on a lightly floured surface, and use to line a 25cm/10 inch loose-bottomed flan tin. Prick the base with a fork and pour in the filling mixture. Bake in a preheated oven at 190°C/375°F/Gas Mark 5 for 30 minutes, or until it is set and golden. Set aside to cool.

2 Make the filling: put the lemon rind and juice, and sugar in a mixing bowl. Break in the eggs and add the egg white. Beat well together and then beat in the cream, ground almonds and cinnamon. The mixture should be thick and smooth.

PREPARATION: 15 MINUTES +
30 MINUTES CHILLING
COOKING: 30 MINUTES
SERVES: 6-8

250g/8oz plain flour
pinch of salt
125g/4oz butter
1 egg yolk
2-3 tablespoons iced water
For the filling:
grated rind and juice of 3 lemons
75g/3oz caster sugar
2 eggs + 1 egg white
75ml/3 fl oz double cream
125g/4oz ground almonds
good pinch of ground cinnamon
For the topping:
2 lemons, thinly sliced
125g/4oz caster sugar

4 Heat the lemon slices in a little water over low heat for 10 minutes, or until tender. Remove and drain the lemon slices, keeping about 75ml/3 fl oz of the liquid. Add the sugar and stir over gentle heat until dissolved. Bring to the boil, add the lemon slices and cook rapidly until they are well coated with thick syrup. Remove and use to decorate the tart. Leave to cool and serve.

SAUCES AND PASTRY

AIOLI
Garlic sauce

8 cloves garlic, peeled
salt
2 egg yolks
300ml/½ pint olive oil
freshly ground black pepper
few drops of lemon juice

Crush the garlic with a little salt in a mortar. Place the egg yolks in a bowl and beat with the garlic. Add the olive oil, drop by drop, beating well between each addition. When the mixture thickens and becomes more creamy, you can add the remaining oil in a thin steady stream, beating all the time. Add a little ground black pepper and lemon juice and check the seasoning. You can store the aioli for a few days in a screwtop jar or sealed container in the refrigerator. Makes 300ml/½ pint.

VINAIGRETTE
French oil and vinegar dressing

6 tablespoons olive oil
2 tablespoons white wine vinegar
1 teaspoon Dijon mustard
pinch of sugar
salt and freshly ground black pepper

Put the olive oil and wine vinegar in a bowl and mix with a fork. Whisk in the mustard and sugar until the mixture is thoroughly blended. Season with salt and pepper, and use as a dressing for salads and warm vegetables.

Variation: if liked, you can omit the mustard, or add crushed garlic or chopped fresh herbs of your choice.

ROUILLE
Red pepper sauce

1 small red pepper
2 garlic cloves, crushed
pinch of saffron powder
salt and freshly ground black pepper
50g/2oz crustless white bread
2 egg yolks
250ml/8 fl oz olive oil

Cut the pepper in half and remove the core and seeds. Chop the flesh into small pieces and crush to a paste with the garlic in a mortar. Add the saffron and salt and pepper to taste. Moisten the bread with a little water or some of the cooking liquid if making bouillabaisse (the traditional accompaniment for rouille). Work it into the peppers and garlic until thoroughly incorporated. Beat in the egg yolks. Add the oil, a little at a time, beating well between each addition. As the rouille becomes thick, pour the oil in a thin steady stream. Continue beating until the rouille is thick and smooth. Makes 250ml/8 fl oz.

PATE BRISEE
Shortcrust pastry

250g/8oz plain flour
75g/3oz butter, cut into small pieces
1 egg
pinch of salt
4–6 tablespoons water
50g/2oz sugar(optional)

Sift the flour into a large bowl, and rub in the butter with your fingertips until the mixture resembles fine breadcrumbs.

Add the egg, salt and sufficient water to mix to a soft dough. If making sweet pastry for a fruit pie or flan, you can mix in the sugar and some extra water. Wrap the dough in polythene and rest in the refrigerator for at least 30 minutes before using. The dough can be stored in this way in the refrigerator for up to 2 days.

Note: alternatively, the pastry can be made in a food processor.

SAUCE BEARNAISE
Creamy tarragon sauce

250g/8oz butter, cut into small pieces
7 tablespoons white wine vinegar
2 shallots, finely chopped
¼ teaspoon freshly ground white pepper
2 tablespoons chopped tarragon
3 egg yolks
2 tablespoons water
salt

Clarify the butter (as described in the recipe for sauce hollandaise). Put the vinegar in a saucepan with the shallots, pepper and half of the tarragon. Boil rapidly until the liquid has reduced to 1 tablespoon. Strain the reduced liquid into a clean pan and stand it in a water bath *(bain marie)*.

Add the egg yolks to the strained liquid, one at a time, whisking vigorously. Whisk in the water, and then the clarified butter, a little at a time, until the sauce is like thick cream. Add the remaining tarragon and salt to taste. Serve with grilled steak or roast beef.

SAUCE HOLLANDAISE

250g/8oz butter, cut into small pieces
2 tablespoons white wine vinegar
4 tablespoons water
¼ teaspoon freshly ground white pepper
3 egg yolks
1-2 tablespoons lemon juice
salt

First clarify the butter: put it in a heavy pan and melt over very low heat. Skim off the white foam that rises to the surface, and strain the clear yellow liquid into a bowl.

Put the vinegar in a heavy pan with 2 tablespoons of water and the white pepper. Boil rapidly until the liquid has reduced to 1 teaspoon. Remove from the heat and stand the pan in a larger saucepan or a roasting pan half-filled with water (a *bain marie*). Stir 1 tablespoon of water into the reduced liquid and then add the egg yolks, one at a time, whisking vigorously after each addition.

Whisk in the clarified butter, a little at a time. Then whisk in the remaining water. The consistency of the sauce should be like thick cream. Pass the sauce through a sieve or conical strainer and then whisk in the lemon juice and salt to taste. Serve with cooked fish dishes and vegetables, especially asparagus.

Variation: to make a sauce mousseline, fold 2 tablespoons of lightly whipped cream into the hollandaise sauce just before serving.

BECHAMEL SAUCE
White sauce

600ml/1 pint milk
1 onion stuck with 2 cloves
1 carrot, quartered
bouquet garni
50g/2oz butter
50g/2oz flour
salt and freshly ground white pepper
freshly grated nutmeg

Pour the milk into a saucepan and add the onion, carrot and bouquet garni. Bring to the boil and then reduce the heat to a bare simmer. Leave the saucepan over very low heat for 30 minutes to infuse. Melt the butter in a clean saucepan and stir in the flour. Cook for 1 minute, stirring constantly to obtain a smooth roux (paste). Do not allow the roux to brown. Remove the pan from the heat and gradually stir in the milk, a little at a time, stirring vigorously after each addition. The sauce should be smooth without any lumps. Return to the heat and bring slowly to the boil, stirring constantly. Lower the heat and simmer gently for 5-6 minutes until the sauce thickens. Season with salt, pepper and grated nutmeg.

Variation: vary the flavour by adding chopped fresh herbs, such as tarragon, parsley or chervil. Or you can add up to 300ml/½ pint freshly made tomato sauce for a sauce aurore to serve with fish, chicken and egg dishes.

MAYONNAISE

1 egg yolk
125-150ml/4-5 fl oz olive oil
pinch of salt
3-4 teaspoons white wine vinegar or lemon juice

Before you make the mayonnaise, ensure that all the ingredients and utensils are at room temperature. Put the egg yolk in a bowl and beat with a whisk. Add the olive oil to the egg yolk, drop by drop at first, beating all the time. As the mayonnaise starts to thicken, start adding the oil faster in a thin, steady stream. Continue beating throughout until all the oil is absorbed. Add salt to taste, and blend in the vinegar or lemon juice. Serve at room temperature. Makes 150ml/¼ pint mayonnaise

Variation: if you like a mustard-flavoured mayonnaise, add 1 teaspoon Dijon mustard to the egg yolk before adding the olive oil.

Important: if the mayonnaise starts to curdle, quickly whisk in 1 tablespoon boiling water. If this does not do the trick, you can start again with another egg yolk in a clean bowl. Add the curdled mayonnaise mixture, one drop at a time, beating well. Add the remaining olive oil drop by drop and then in a thin stream.

INDEX